basix™

Recorder Method

Morty Manus

Get Down to BASIX™!

BASIX™ is all you need to take off with your instrument. Alfred has worked hard to help you begin learning today with our easy-to-use, comprehensive series. It won't frustrate you by moving too fast, or let you get bored by moving too slow! You'll notice pics of many great performers; we added those to fire your imagination and help you stay focused on becoming a star yourself! To top it off, you can put what you learn to work when you play along with the companion CD. Set your sights high by beginning with BASIX™... the series that will get you there!

D1303648

Cover photo courtesy of Yamaha.

2

CONTENTS

FOREWORD

This book shows you how to master the basic skills of playing the recorder. Even if you do not read music or have never played an instrument before, the step-by-step instructions will soon have you playing real songs and enjoying the charming and intimate sounds of this most ancient, yet modern, instrument. Along with clear illustrations and explanations of fingering, you'll learn how to read music by playing songs from every period of music history, from the 16th-century beauty of *Greensleeves* to today's *When the Saints Go Marching In, Amazing Grace, La Bamba, This Land is Your Land* and dozens of others.

You'll be amazed how quickly your playing skills will develop as you go through the page-by-page explorations of this sweetest sounding woodwind instrument.

ABOUT THE RECORDER

The musical instrument known as the recorder has been the most widely-played of all serious instruments from as long ago as 1400 until the present. It has been popular in many cultures, not only with professional musicians, but also with adult amateurs and especially with children. Playing the recorder can be very satisfying, as it is not only inexpensive, but easier to master than most other instruments.

Recorders can be seen on display in museums. Many of the ancient instruments are very beautiful, fashioned from ivory, ebony, or other precious materials and sometimes elaborately carved with intricate inlaid patterns. Recorders come in many different sizes, from the tiny sopranino to the huge "big bass." They are constructed in a tube shape, one end of which is partially closed and shaped to form a whistle-like mouthpiece. The player's breath is directed through the narrow channel and across a small opening, creating vibrations which are then transmitted through the air in the tube. The pitch of the vibrations is changed mostly by covering and uncovering the thumb and finger holes, and partly by overblowing.

In the earliest times a recorder player might accompany a singer or troubadour. It was a favorite for background music in dramatic presentations and was used to imitate birds for pastoral scenes. Its pure tones enhanced scenes of love, miraculous happenings onstage, appearances of gods and goddesses, and brought an added solemnity to funeral scenes.

King Henry VIII of England (1491–1547) so loved playing and listening to recorders that he owned over 70 of them. In one of his plays, Shakespeare has Hamlet describing how to play the recorder. Great composers like Bach, Purcell, Handel and Vivaldi wrote for it. Until the late 18th century it was the woodwind of choice in the orchestras of that time. But the perfection of the key mechanism on the flute made that instrument far superior to the recorder, both in volume as well as the ability to negotiate difficult chromatic passages. This caused the recorder to fall into disuse for over a hundred years.

Then, during the first World War, the recorder was rediscovered. Because other instruments were scarce, schools resorted to using recorders to teach music. Although the traditional techniques for playing had been lost during the 19th century, teachers began to rediscover the intimate charm of the recorder's delicate and sweet sound.

Today the recorder is once more at the height of popularity. It is easy to learn, reasonably priced, and appropriate for many kinds of music, from the Renaissance, baroque, and classical literature of its early period, to the folk and pop songs of today.

WHO THIS BOOK IS FOR

Whether or not you already read music, whether you are a young person learning a first instrument, an adult beginner, a senior looking for a new hobby or if you just want to regain lost musical skills, you will find this a valuable book. It tells you all you need to know to master the basic skills of playing the recorder and reading music on that instrument. All you need is a recorder, this book, a little time and perseverance, and very soon you'll be enjoying the charming, intimate sound of this ancient, yet very modern, instrument.

CHOOSING AN INSTRUMENT

Recorders come in a variety of sizes from small and high-pitched to large and deep. The four most popular sizes are soprano (or descant—about 12-1/2 inches long), alto (about 18 inches long), tenor (about 25 inches long), and bass (about 36 inches long). The longer the tube, the lower the notes it plays. Less used are the sopranino, which is smaller and higher than the soprano, and the big bass, which is larger and deeper than the bass.

The most important thing about choosing the right sized instrument is making sure it will match the size of your hand. Try a soprano first. Can you cover all the holes easily? Most people with average-sized hands can, and this is why the soprano is the most popular size. Even young children have no trouble reaching the holes on this sweet-sounding instrument. The tenor and bass might better be left for another time after you have mastered the basic techniques of playing the smaller recorders. You won't have lost anything, because all recorders use the same fingering.

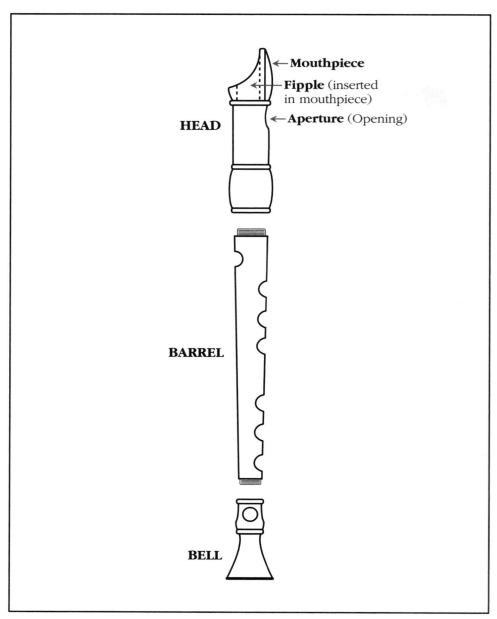

▲ *Parts of the recorder.*

CARING FOR THE RECORDER

If you have a wooden recorder, warm it with your hands and breathe into it before playing. Always swab it out after playing to get rid of any moisture. If you're playing one of the larger instruments, use a little cork grease when assembling it. The sections should fit together firmly, but without forcing. And, of course, never expose your recorder to extremes of heat or cold.

HOW TO HOLD THE RECORDER

As you can see from the photograph, the left hand is placed closer to the mouthpiece. The index, middle and ring fingers are used to cover the first three holes on top of the recorder. The thumb covers the one hole underneath.

Four fingers are used on the right hand. Notice that the lowest hole is placed a little off center to make it easier to reach with the pinky. On the right hand, the thumb does not cover any holes, but is used to help support the instrument.

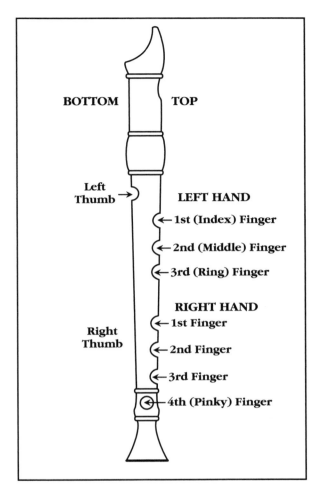

PRODUCING A TONE

Place the mouthpiece between your lips. Blow softly. If you blow too hard, the tone will crack. To start the tone, lightly place the tip of your tongue just behind your upper front teeth and quickly remove it. By saying the syllable "tu," your tongue will automatically be placed in the correct position. This is called **tonguing**. Take a breath and use your tongue to start and stop the tone.

HOW TO PRACTICE

Today, many people are pressed for time, so it is important to get the most of your practice. Consider getting a metronome. These devices have come a long way from the "tick-tock" pendulum type familiar to every music student. Today's electronic metronomes can be purchased inexpensively, and can be set to keep a steady beat anywhere between 40 to over 200 beats per minute. Practicing with a metronome gives you the discipline to play accurately and smoothly—the sure mark of a professional-quality player.

At first, don't overpractice. Start with a 15-minute repetition of the material you're working on. Within a few weeks, lengthen this to 30 minutes and eventually to 45 minutes per day. Of course, you can play longer than this, but don't forget to enjoy yourself. Play songs. Compose your own tunes. Have fun.

GETTING ACQUAINTED WITH MUSIC

Notes are the basic units of music. They tell you two things: what pitch to play (melody) and how long to play it (rhythm). There are several types of notes—open, open with stems, closed with stems, and closed with stems and flags (see diagram 1).

Written music tells you what pitch to play by placing notes on a five-line **staff** (see diagram 2). The notes are named by letters: A B C D E F G. No other letters are used.

In order to identify the notes on the five-line staff, a symbol called a **clef** is placed at the beginning of each staff. Music for the recorder is written in the **treble clef**. The treble clef symbol is derived from the Gothic letter G:

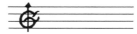

The modern clef still shows the position of the note G by curling around the second line of the staff, the place where G is written.

Bar lines are vertical lines that divide the staff into **measures** (see diagram 3). This shows the basic pulse of the music and makes reading music easier by dividing the notes into shorter groups.

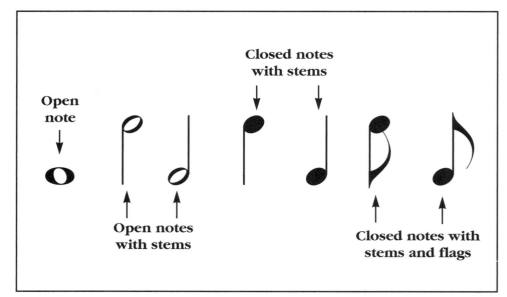

▲ 1. *Various types of notes.*

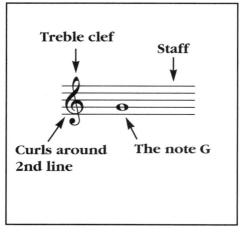

▲ 2. *The five-line staff with treble clef*

▼ 3. *Measures and bar lines.*

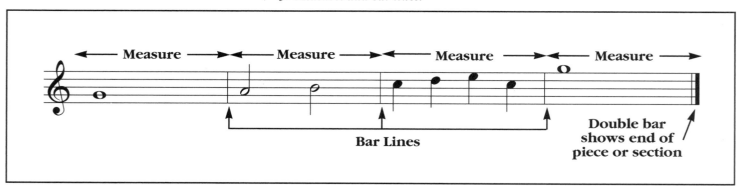

NAMING THE NOTES

Notes are placed on the five-line staff either in the spaces or on the lines.

Notes in the spaces

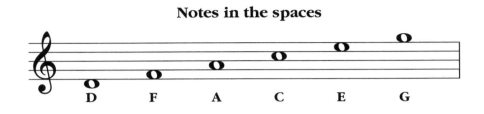

Notes on the lines

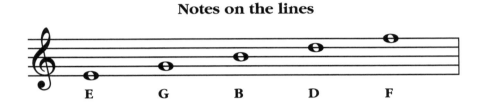

The following memory tricks will help you identify the notes:

In the spaces: **D**on't **F**orget, **A**ll **C**ows **E**at **G**rass

On the lines: **E**very **G**ood **B**oy **D**oes **F**ine

Identify the following notes and write their names in the spaces provided below each staff.

In the spaces

1.

On the lines

2.

In order

3.

In random order

4.
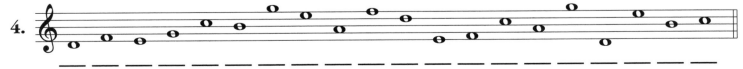

The answers are on page 63.

RHYTHM: QUARTER, HALF, DOTTED HALF, AND WHOLE NOTES

As we have seen, the pitch of a note (how high or low it is) is indicated by its position on the five-line staff. The duration of a note (how long it sounds) is indicated by its shape. Imagine a steady beat, like a clock ticking. Tap your foot to this steady beat. Now blow into your recorder without covering any of the finger or thumb holes. Blow once for each down-beat or foot tap. These notes are called **quarter notes** and look like this:

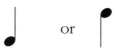

Half notes last for two beats and look like this:

Dotted half notes last for three beats and look like this:

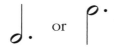

Whole notes last for four beats and look like this:

o

Play the following rhythmic exercises by blowing gently into your recorder. Use the syllable "tu" and hold each note for the correct number of beats. Tongue each note on the down-beat. Do not cover any of the finger or thumb holes.

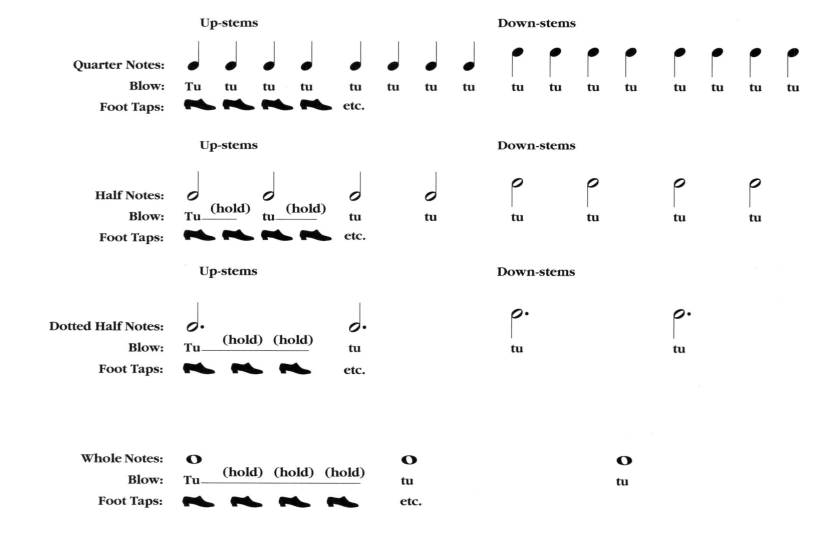

Playing the Note B

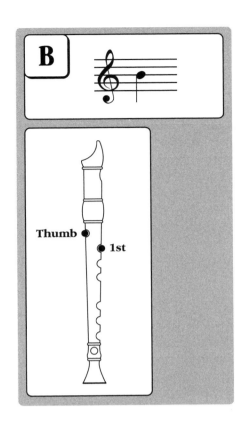

B

As this note requires the use of only the thumb and one finger on the left hand, it is one of the easiest notes to play on the recorder. Study the diagram carefully and then blow gently into the mouthpiece using the syllable "tu" to start the sound.

Thumb ●
● 1st

Tongue each note. Make certain that you have covered the two holes completely. Be careful that you do not cover any other holes accidentally. Support the recorder with your right hand thumb.

⸴ means to take a breath.

B	B	B_____ ⸴	B	B	B_____ ⸴	B_____	B_____ ⸴	B	B	B ___
Tu	tu	tu___(hold)	tu	tu	tu_____	tu_____	tu_____	tu	tu	tu___

Keep the pattern of notes as above: short-short-long, short-short-long, long-long, short-short-long. (Short means one beat or tap of your foot; long means two beats or taps of your foot.)

Track 1 In musical notation what you have just played looks like this:

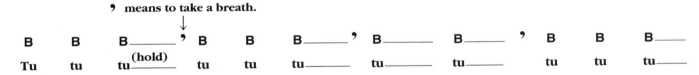

Short   short   long_____ ,   short   short   long_____ ,   long_____   long_____ ,   short   short   long_____.

Here's another pattern to try:

B	B	B	B ⸴	B	B	B___ ⸴	B___	B	B ⸴	B___	B	B ⸴	B___	B ___
Tu	tu	tu	tu	tu	tu	tu___	tu___	tu	tu	tu___	tu	tu	tu___	tu ___

Track 2 In musical notation:

Short   short   short   short,   short   short   long,   long   short short,   long   short short,   long   long.

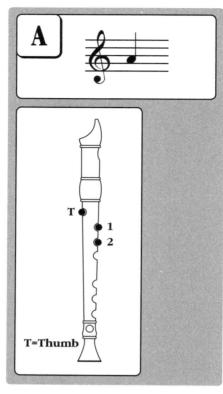

Playing the Note A

As you can see from the diagram, the note A requires that you cover the thumb hole and the top two finger holes with your left hand. Again, blow gently into the mouthpiece while pronouncing the syllable "tu." Tongue each note as you play. The note A sounds lower than B and is written lower on the staff.

If you're not getting a steady, even sound, make sure your fingers are covering the appropriate holes *completely*. Even a tiny space around the hole will produce the wrong note or a high-pitched squeak.

Tap your foot evenly—one tap for each quarter note (♩), two taps for each half note (♩).

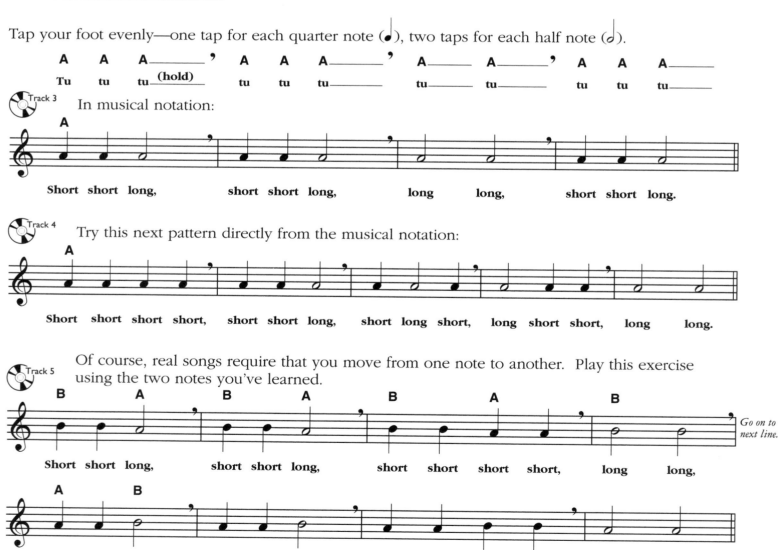

Playing the Note G

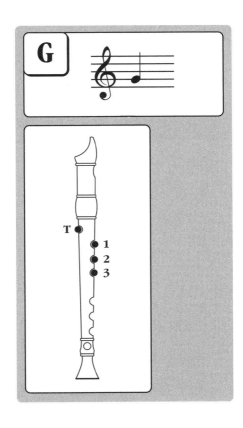

As you can see from the diagram, the note G requires that you cover the thumb hole as well as the top three finger holes. Tap your foot evenly—one tap for each quarter note (♩), two taps for each half note (♩). Take deeper breaths so that you can play two measures without breathing. Tongue each note.

Short short short short, long long, long short short, short short long.

If the sound keeps breaking up, you're blowing too hard. Soft and steady gets the best sound!

It's in the B-A-G

Track 6

Short short long,

Merrily We Roll Along

Track 7

METER: MEASURES AND TIME SIGNATURES

As mentioned on page 6, music is divided into **measures** of equal numbers of beats. At the beginning of each piece of music, you'll find a fraction called a **time signature**. The upper number of the fraction tells you how many beats are contained within each measure. For example, a measure of 4/4 time (say: four quarter time) always contains four beats. Here are a few possibilities: (Play these examples on the note G.)

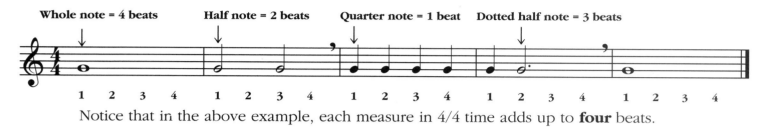

Notice that in the above example, each measure in 4/4 time adds up to **four** beats.

A measure in 3/4 (three quarter time) always adds up to **three** beats.

A measure in 2/4 (two quarter time) always adds up to **two** beats.

Here are some examples in each time signature. Remember to tongue each note with "tu."

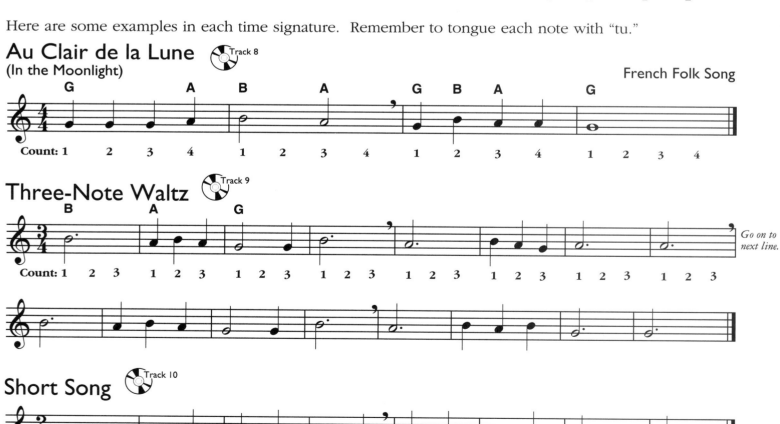

Au Clair de la Lune
(In the Moonlight)   Track 8

French Folk Song

Three-Note Waltz   Track 9

Go on to next line.

Short Song   Track 10

RESTS: QUARTER, HALF and WHOLE RESTS

When silence is called for in music, a symbol called a **rest** is used. It is important to remember that a rest is a *measured* silence, that is, a silence that lasts for a certain number of beats.

The rests used in music are:

Quarter rest ❳ = 1 beat of silence

Half rest ▬ = 2 beats of silence

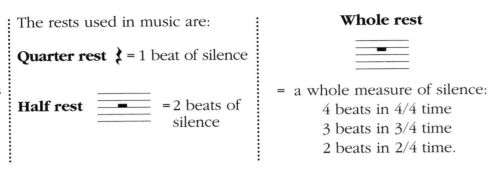

Whole rest

= a whole measure of silence:
  4 beats in 4/4 time
  3 beats in 3/4 time
  2 beats in 2/4 time.

Play the following examples. Keep the beat steady and count all notes and rests carefully. You may take a breath at any rest mark. Continue to tongue each note with "tu."

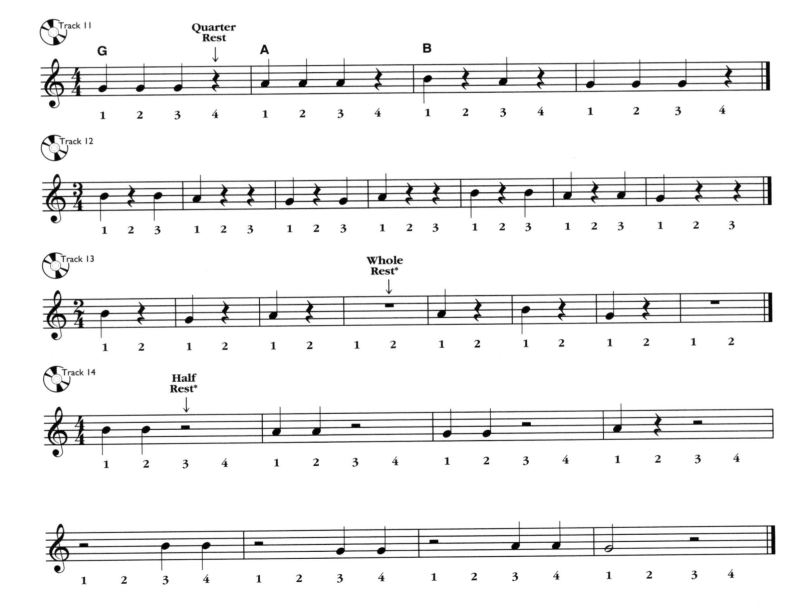

*Here is an easy way to remember the difference between half rests and whole rests: half rests (2 beats) are lighter and so rest on top of the staff line; whole rests (a whole measure of silence) are heavier and so hang from the staff line.

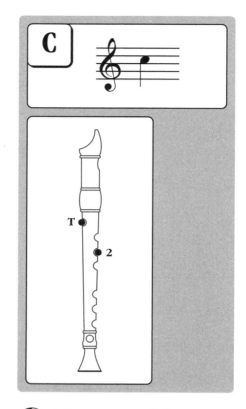

Playing Middle C

As you can see from the diagram, the note C requires only the thumb and one finger of the left hand. Make sure not to overblow this note, as this will make it go out of tune or even break up completely. (The recorder "middle" C differs from middle C on the piano and is used here to refer to the middle of the recorder's range.)

These valuable exercises develop your ability to easily connect the four notes you have learned:

PLAYING WITH G A B C

Bohemian Folk Song — Track 18

A Waltz for You — Track 19

Warming Up to C — Track 20

Playing C and B requires the precise raising and lowering of the 1st and 2nd fingers.

Barcarolle
(from "The Tales of Hoffman") — Track 21

J. Offenbach

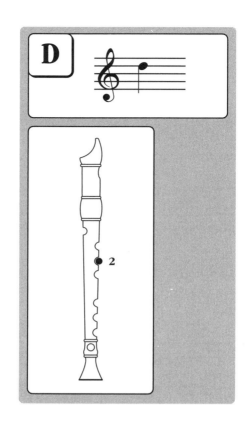

Playing Up to High D

For the first time, a new note does not require you to cover the thumb hole. If your thumb is flexible, rotate it away from the thumb hole, making sure that the hole is completely clear. Otherwise, lift the thumb off the recorder while steadying the instrument with your right hand.

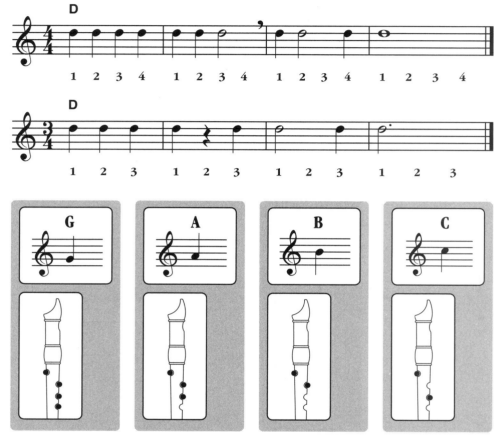

The following exercises will help you to become familiar with the new note D you have just learned and to connect it with the notes you already know. Remember to tongue each note.

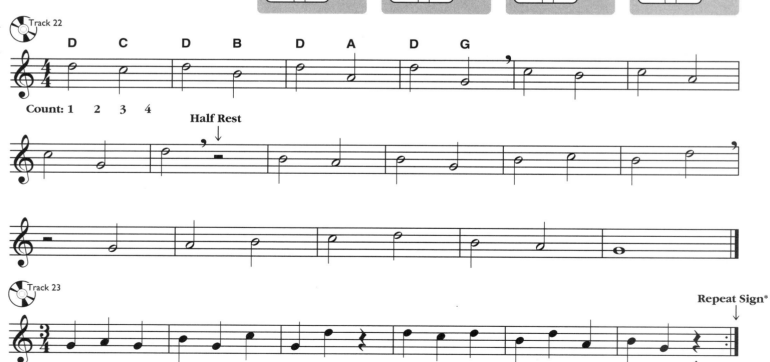

*Go back to the beginning of the exercise and play again.

PLAYING WITH G A B C D

Jingle Bells

Track 24

Quarter Rest

Jin - gle bells, jin - gle bells, jin - gle all the way!

Oh, what fun it is to ride in a one - horse o - pen sleigh, hey!

Jin - gle bells, jin - gle bells, jin - gle all the way!

Oh, what fun it is to ride in a one - horse o - pen sleigh!

I Know Where I'm Going

Track 25

I know where I'm go - ing, I know who's go - ing with me;

I know who I love,_____ And he knows who I'll mar - ry!

Feath - er beds are soft, And paint - ed rooms are bon - ny, But

I would trade them all,_____ for strong and hand - some John - ny.

PLAYING WITH G A B C D (cont'd.)

Good King Wenceslas (first part) — Track 26

Aura Lee (first part)* — Track 27

Elvis Presley recorded this folk song in a modern version called "Love Me Tender."

Beautiful Brown Eyes — Track 28

Beau - ti - ful, beau - ti - ful brown eyes, smil - ing right

in - to my heart. But now where are those beau - ti - ful brown

eyes? Why must we be so far a - part?

*For complete version see page 58.

Go Tell Aunt Rhody

Go tell Aunt Rho - dy, go tell Aunt Rho - dy,

go tell Aunt Rho - dy, the old gray goose is dead.

When the Saints Go Marching In

Oh, when the saints go march - ing in, Oh, when the

saints go march - ing in, Oh Lord, I want to

Half Rest

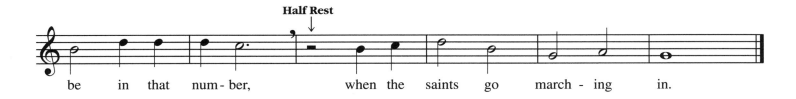

be in that num - ber, when the saints go march - ing in.

Love Somebody

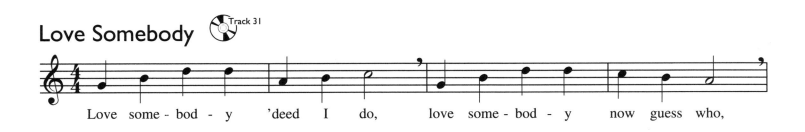

Love some - bod - y 'deed I do, love some - bod - y now guess who,

Love some - bod - y have you guessed, you're the one I love the best.

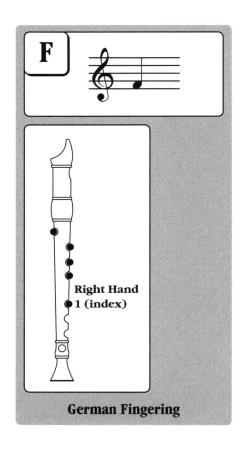

German Fingering

Playing Low F

The note F can be played two different ways. On the left is the so-called German fingering. It is easier to play than the Baroque fingering on the right. However, the German fingering does not give as pure a sound, so if you have very well-coordinated fingers, use the Baroque fingering. Make certain the bell is turned so your 4th finger (pinky) covers the two small double holes. If you have trouble with this fingering, use the German.

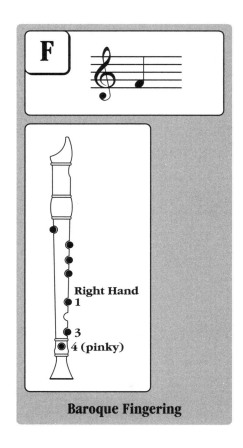

Baroque Fingering

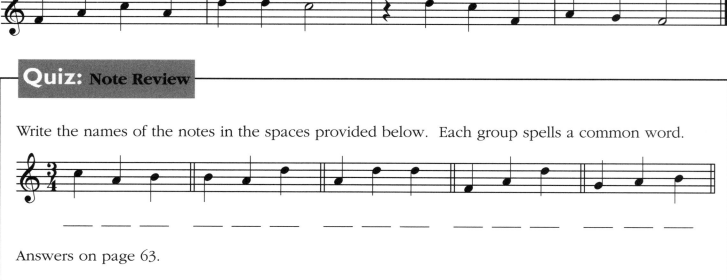

Quiz: Note Review

Write the names of the notes in the spaces provided below. Each group spells a common word.

Answers on page 63.

EIGHTH NOTES

Eighth notes are black notes with a flag added to the stem.

Two or more eighth notes are written.

To count eighth notes, we divide each beat into two parts, calling the 2nd part "and."

Count: 1   &   2   &   3   &   4   &

Track 32

Eighth notes are played twice as fast as quarter notes.
Quarter notes are played twice as fast as half notes.

Repeat Sign

Count: 1   2   3   4   1   2   3   4   1 & 2 & 3 & 4 & 1   2   3   4

Quiz: Eighth Notes

How many eighth notes can you fit into a measure of 2/4 time? _____ 3/4 time? _____ 4/4 time? _____

Add enough eighth notes to complete the following measures (Answers on page 63):

Musette Track 33

J.S. Bach

Count: 1 2 3 & 4 &   1 2 3 & 4 &   1 & 2 3 4   1 2 3 4

1 2 3 & 4 &   1 2 3 & 4 &   1 & 2 3 4   1 2 3 4

Up On the Housetop Track 34
(First part)

Traditional

Count: 1 2 & 3 4 &

1 2 & 3 4 &   1 2 & 3 & 4

Shortnin' Bread Track 35

Traditional

Three lit-tle chil-dren ly-ing in bed, Two were sick and the oth-er near dead!

Sent for the doc-tor, doc-tor said, "Feed them chil-dren some short-nin' bread."

Mom-my's lit-tle ba-by loves short-nin', short-nin', Mom-my's lit-tle ba-by loves short-nin' bread.

Mom-my's lit-tle ba-by loves short-nin', short-nin', Mom-my's lit-tle ba-by loves short-nin' bread.

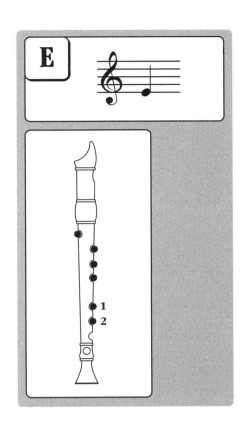

Playing Low E

As you can see from the diagram, low E requires one more finger than the easy F fingering you just learned. This part of the recorder is very logical—the lower you go, the more fingers are required.

Also, remember that it is easy to overblow the low notes, so play softly when in this part of the recorder's *register* (the range: high, low or middle). When tonguing these low notes, try using the syllable "du" and see if it prevents overblowing. "Du" releases your breath a little more gently than "tu."

Here are two very valuable studies that deal with the problems of connecting low E to other notes you have learned. If you are using the Baroque fingering for F, *Connecting E and F* is particularly tricky.

Connecting E and F

Big City Polka

TEMPO SIGNS

Because Italian musicians dominated European music at the time tempo signs first came into general use, we still use Italian words to indicate how slow or fast to play a piece of music. The three most common of these are:

Andante (on-DON-tay) = slow;

Moderato (mod-er-AH-to) = moderately;

Allegro (a-LAY-grow) = fast.

Many modern editions, especially those oriented toward popular music, use English words such as "slow ballad," "moderate ragtime tempo," "bright rock," etc.

Big City Blues

When playing blues or jazz it is very effective to play the eighth notes unevenly, called "swinging." Play the notes long-short, long-short, rather than an even 1 & 2 &.

*D.C. al Fine stands for "Da Capo al Fine," an Italian phrase meaning to repeat from the beginning and play through to the word *fine* (end). In the example above, play measures 1 through 16, then play measures 1 through 8 again.

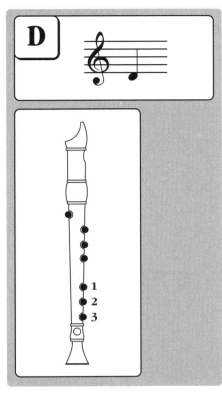

Playing Low D

As you approach the lowest notes of the recorder, more and more fingers are required to cover the holes. As you can see from the diagram, you'll need the thumb and three fingers of the left hand as well as three fingers of the right hand to play low D. Depending on your instrument and shape of your mouth, you may have to slightly lower your jaw to play the lower notes of the recorder. All holes must be closed completely to sound the note correctly.

Do not confuse this D with the high D that you learned on page 16. Although they have the same name, the higher D is eight notes above the low D. In music this is called an octave higher.

Connections Track 39

Octave Waltz Track 40

PICKUPS

Sometimes a song begins with an incomplete measure called a **pickup**. The pickup measure contains fewer beats than are called for in the time signature. For example, a 4/4 pickup measure may contain one, two or three beats. A 3/4 measure may contain one or two beats, and so on. Even partial beats can be used, which we'll discuss later in the book.

Often (but not always) the last measure of the piece will be missing the same number of beats that the pickup uses. In this way the initial incomplete measure is completed.

Below are some short excerpts of familiar tunes that show pickups of various numbers of beats in 2/4, 3/4 and 4/4 time.

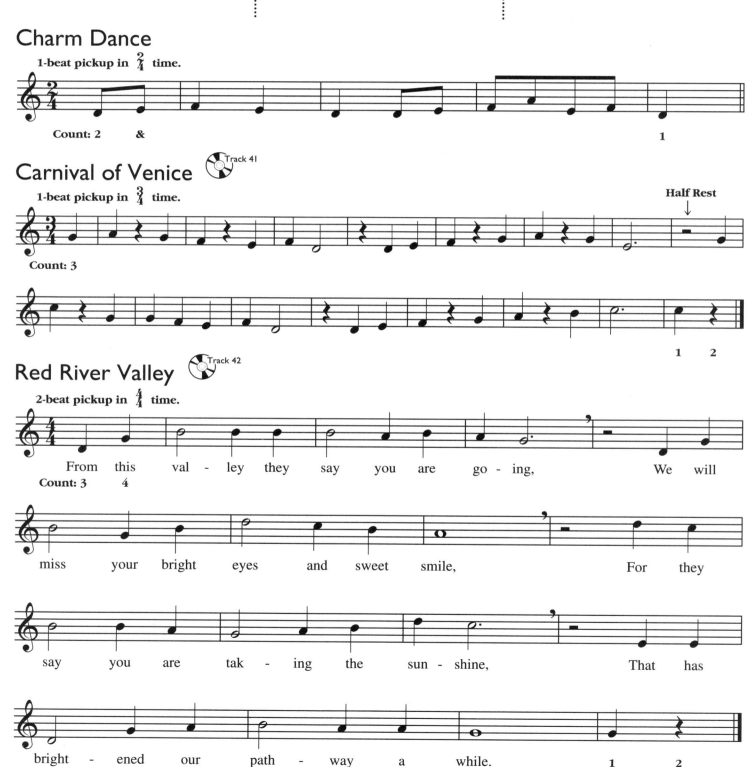

Charm Dance

1-beat pickup in 2/4 time.

Count: 2   &   1

Carnival of Venice   Track 41

1-beat pickup in 3/4 time.

Half Rest

Count: 3

1   2

Red River Valley   Track 42

2-beat pickup in 4/4 time.

From this val - ley they say you are go - ing,   We will

Count: 3   4

miss your bright eyes and sweet smile,   For they

say you are tak - ing the sun - shine,   That has

bright - ened our path - way a while.   1   2

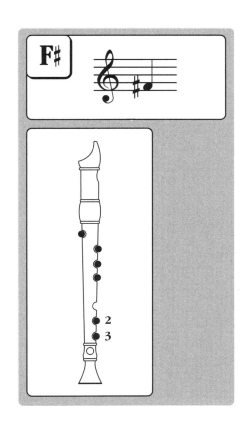

Playing F Sharp

The **sharp** symbol ♯ is used to show that a note has been raised. In this case the note F♯ (say: F sharp) lies between F and G.

It is a very important note on the recorder, and occurs in many of the melodies you will play.

As you can see from the diagram, the fingering does not present any unusual challenge.

A sharp carries over through the entire measure, so if other F's appear in a measure after an F♯, they are also played as sharps.

Also played as F♯

F♯ Study

Still F♯

It Ain't Gonna Rain

Track 43

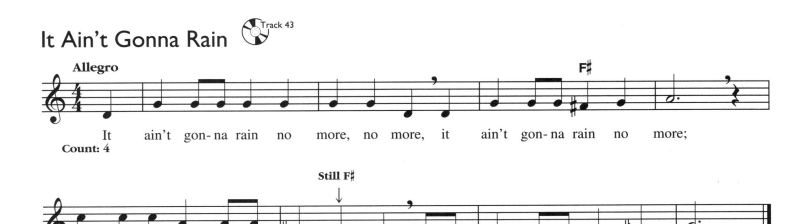

Allegro

It ain't gon-na rain no more, no more, it ain't gon-na rain no more;

Count: 4

Still F♯

How in the heck can I wash my neck if it ain't gon-na rain no more?

1   2   3

Down in the Valley  Track 44

Appalachian Folk Song

Moderato

Down in the val - ley, val - ley so low,

Hang your head o - ver, hear the wind blow.

Hear the wind blow, boys, hear the wind blow,

Hang your head o - ver, hear the wind blow.

I Love You Truly Track 45

This sentimental favorite from the early 1900s is still sung at weddings.

Andante

I love you tru - ly, tru - ly, dear.

Life with its sor - row, life with its tear,

fades in - to dreams when I feel you are near,

for I love you tru - ly, tru - ly, dear.

KEY SIGNATURES

On the previous two songs, "Down in the Valley" and "I Love You Truly," you may have noticed that **every F was played as F♯**. When this occurs in a song, musicians use a shortcut called a **key signature**. This is one or more sharps placed immediately after each clef.

In the next song the key signature consists of one sharp placed on the F line of the staff. This means that **every F in the piece is played as F♯**. We'll remind you a few times when F appears, but most music does not do this, so it'll be up to you to remember.

Ordinarily a piece with an F♯ key signature is said to be in the key of G major.

Oh Come, All Ye Faithful

(Adeste Fideles)

Christmas Carol

TIES

A **tie** is symbolized by a curved line that connects two or more notes of the same pitch. Tied notes are not played separately, but their values are added together. For example, two tied quarter notes would be held for two beats. A half note tied to a whole note would be held for six beats. Three whole notes tied together would last for twelve beats and so on.

Below are various examples of tied notes in 2/4, 3/4 and 4/4 time. Practice them making sure to keep a steady beat and to count carefully.

When the note stems go down, the tie curves above the note.

When the note stem goes up, the tie curves below the note.

Ode to Joy

Track 47

Beethoven

Quiz: Ties

As you know, whole notes are held for four beats, dotted half notes for three beats, half notes for two beats, quarter notes for one beat, and eighth notes for half a beat. For how many beats are the following tied groups held? Answers on page 63.

1.

2.

3.

This Land Is Your Land

Track 48

Woody Guthrie

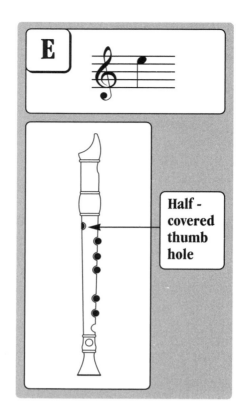

E

Half - covered thumb hole

Playing High E

High E introduces a new technique, that of half covering a hole. The fingering for high E is the same as for low E except that the thumb hole is half covered. If your thumb is flexible, rotate it partly off the hole and blow a little harder than for the low E. If you have trouble rotating the thumb to half uncover the hole, slide it to the side to partially open it.

In the following octave study, only the thumb has to move. This is because the left- and right-hand fingers are otherwise identical when playing the low E and high E.

A Short Study on High E

There's a Hole in the Bucket Track 49

American Folk Song

There's a hole in the buck - et, dear Li - za, dear Li - za, there's a

hole in the buck - et, dear Li - za, a hole.

THE FERMATA (⌢), REPEAT SIGNS AND 1st & 2nd ENDINGS

The symbol ⌢ which classical musicians call a "fermata" and pop musicians call a "bird's eye" or "hold" means to hold the note under it a little longer than usual, at the player's discretion.

"My Wild Irish Rose" on page 33 introduces the use of repeat signs with 1st and 2nd endings. These are space-saving devices that allow musicians to put more material in less space. Repeat signs can face either forward ‖: or backward :‖.

When you see a backward-facing repeat sign, immediately skip back to the forward-facing one. For example, look at "My Wild Irish Rose." Notice the repeat signs. One is facing forward at measure 1, while the other is facing back at measure 16. Play this song by starting with the quarter note pickup (G), playing through measures 1 through 16; go back to the forward-facing repeat sign at measure 1 and play measures 1 through 11 again; skip the material under the 1st ending (measures 12 through 16) and play the measures in the 2nd ending (17 through 21) instead. You will have played a total of 32 measures in all.

THE STACCATO DOT

When a dot appears directly above or below a note:

it means to cut that note off short. The musical term for this is the Italian word *staccato* (stuh-CAH-to). On the recorder, this effect is produced by quickly pronouncing the syllable "tut" or "dut" into the mouthpiece.

Play the following using the note B:

Tu   tu   tu   tu   tut tut tut tut   tu   tu   tu   tu   tut tut tut tut

The following march, "Colonel Bogey," was used in the film "Bridge on the River Kwai." It makes use of the staccato in quite a few places.

Colonel Bogey Track 52

Kenneth J. Alford

DOTTED QUARTER NOTES

Placing a dot after a note increases its value by half. For example, placing a dot after a half note (which is held for two beats) increases its value by half, so a dotted half note is held for three beats.

Placing a dot after a quarter note (which is held for one beat) increases its value by half, so a dotted quarter note is held for one-and-a-half beats. A dotted quarter note is usually followed by an eighth note.

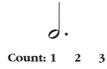

Count: 1　2　3

Count: 1　&　2　&

The next two lines show two different ways of notating the same rhythm.

Here are some fragments of familiar tunes that use the dotted quarter rhythm:

All Through the Night

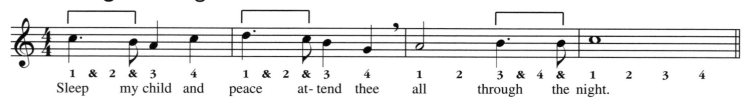

Green Grow Grow the Lilacs

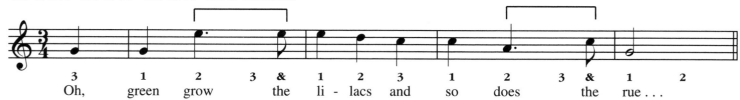

My Country 'Tis of Thee

SONGS THAT USE THE DOTTED QUARTER NOTE

If you're having trouble with the dotted quarter rhythm, mark the dot by tapping your foot like this:

This will help keep the rhythm coordinated with the beat.

Michael Row the Boat Ashore Track 53

Sea Island Folk Song

Auld Lang Syne Track 54

Words by Robert Burns
Music Traditional

THE EIGHTH REST

The symbol ❼ is used to indicate an 8th rest. This symbol means to leave a silence the length of an eighth note, that is, a half beat.

When eighth notes appear alone, they look like: ♪ or ♪.

Single eighth notes are often used with eighth rests: **Count: 1 & 2 &**

Eighth rests are also used with beamed eighth notes: **1 & 2 &**

Clap or tap the following rhythm: **Count: 1 & 2 & 3 & 4 & 1 & 2 & 3 & 4 &**

On the recorder, eighth notes followed by eighth rests are played by pronouncing the syllable "tut" or "dut" into the mouthpiece.

Tut	dut	tut	tut	tut	tut	tu		tut	tut	tut	tut	tu		tu	
1	2	3	4	1	2	3	4	1	2	3	4	1	2	3	4

Eighth rests may also appear on downbeats (the first beat in a measure). This creates no unusual difficulty if you **mark the downbeat by tapping your foot** or by counting mentally.

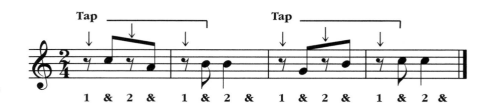

1 & 2 & 1 & 2 & 1 & 2 & 1 & 2 &

Practice the following rhythmic exercises on any note. Make sure to count accurately and to mark unplayed downbeats with a foot tap. Use the note B.

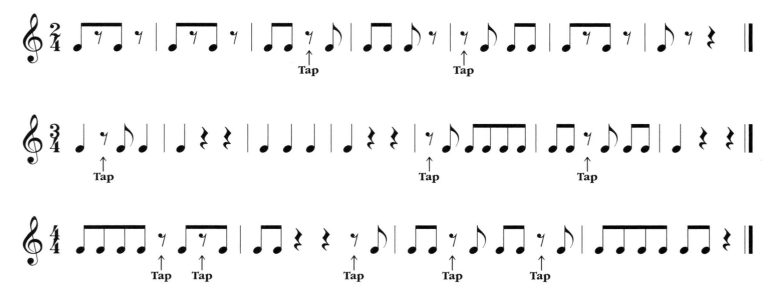

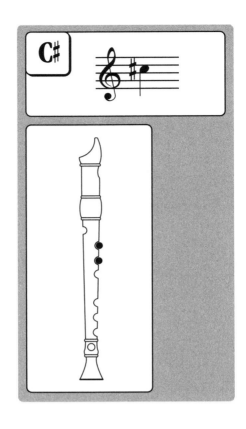

Playing Middle C Sharp

As you can see from the diagram, middle C♯ requires that you uncover the thumb hole and then cover two holes with the left hand. (As mentioned earlier, this "middle" C♯ does not correspond with the piano.)

Middle C♯ allows us to use another key signature. This one has two sharps.

This means that every F is played as F♯ and every C is played as C♯ unless preceded by a **natural sign** ♮.

Ordinarily, music with a two-sharp key signature is said to be in the key of D major.

This famous piece from "Orpheus in the Underworld" should be played briskly and with great spirit. Remember, it is in the key of D, which means that all the F's and C's are played as F♯'s and C♯ 's.

Can-Can Track 55

Jacques Offenbach

THE D MAJOR SCALE

The D major scale arranges all the notes in the key of D in order. Practicing this scale every day will give you facility playing songs in the key of D and will benefit your technique in other ways as well. Remember that the F's and C's are sharped.

Track 56

This famous Christmas song uses the D major scale throughout. Especially notice the opening phrase which uses the descending D major scale note-for-note.

Joy to the World

Track 57

Words by Issac Watts
Music by Lowell Mason

Joy to the world! the Lord is come; Let earth re -

ceive her King; Let ev - 'ry___ heart_____ pre -

pare___ Him___ room,_____ And Heav'n and na - ture___ sing, And___

Heav'n and na - ture___ sing, And___ Heav'n,___ and Heav'n_____ and

na - ture sing.   na - ture sing.

SYNCOPATION

Syncopation is the name given to a musical effect in which a note is anticipated—that is, played before the beat. For example, the following rhythm is not syncopated; each quarter note falls in the expected place, *on* the beat.

The following example uses syncopation. The 3rd quarter note is played on the "and" of the 2nd beat, rather than its expected place on the 3rd beat. For best results, count carefully and **accent** (> = play a little louder) all syncopated notes.

Since the days of ragtime in the late 19th century, syncopation has been an important component in every kind of American music—Dixieland, swing, rock, blues, country and folk—and is also very important in all of the Latin and Caribbean styles such as rhumba, cha-cha, bossa nova, reggae, calypso, ska and salsa. Although a thorough study of syncopation is beyond the scope of this book, the exercises below will introduce you to this essential subject.

In the examples that follow, an unsyncopated measure is followed by a syncopated one. Count carefully and remember to accent the syncopated note. These examples can be played on any note. After you're comfortable with the rhythm, you can make up your own tunes using these syncopations.

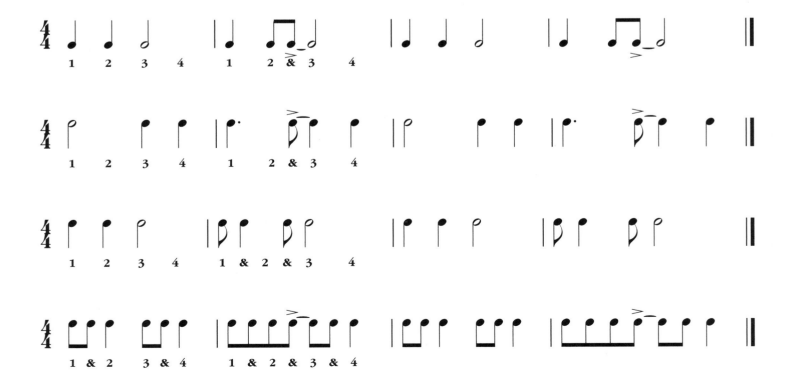

CALYPSO

Calypso music is derived from chants used in various West African cultures as a means of social commentary and satire. It came to the Caribbean region many years ago, and became popular in the U.S. during the '50s, primarily through the music of Harry Belafonte.

Calypso melodies are always highly syncopated, as this famous tune illustrates.

Choucounne Track 58

Traditional

Syncopation also plays an important role in rock, as this bass lick from the '50s shows. From now on, always check the key signature to see what notes are to be sharped. No reminders will be added to the music.

Track 59

% Means to repeat the previous measure

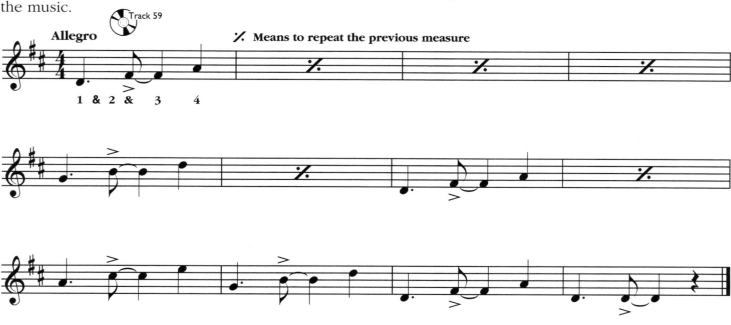

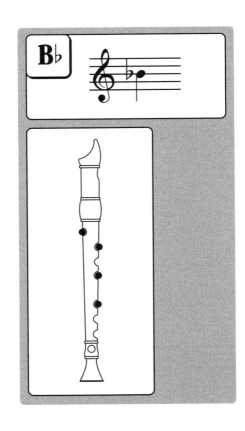

Playing B Flat

The **flat** symbol ♭ is used to mean a note has been lowered. In this case the note B♭ (say: B flat) lies between B and A.

Like the F♯ described on page 27, B♭ is a very important note and occurs in many of the melodies you will play on the recorder.

First play the B♭ alone:

Now contrast the B♭ with B and A:

When B♭ appears in the key signature, it means that every B in the piece is played as a B♭ unless preceded by a **natural sign** (♮). A piece of music with B♭ in the key signature is usually said to be in the key of F major.

TWO MELODIES IN F MAJOR

A Tiskit, A Tasket

This children's play party song was Ella Fitzgerald's first and biggest hit when she sang it with the Chick Webb band in a swing version in 1938.

Rakes of Mallow

A famous Irish folk tune that makes use of the staccato dot as well as the key signature of one flat (F major).

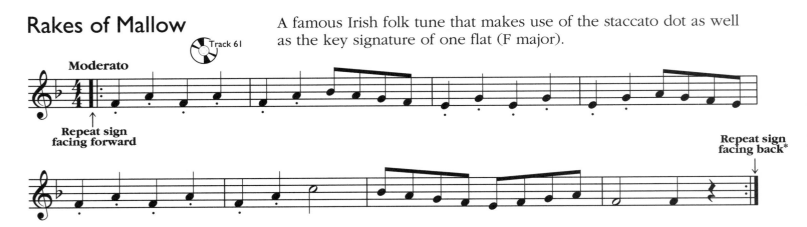

*Note: Music between repeat signs is played twice.

DYNAMICS

Dynamics is the word that musicians use when they want to refer to how *loud* or how *soft* to play. As with many other musical expressions, dynamics are based on Italian words.

From soft . . .		to moderately loud . . .		to very loud, these are:	
pp	*p*	*mp*	*mf*	*f*	*ff*
pianissimo	piano	mezzo piano	mezzo forte	forte	fortissimo.
(pyanISSimo)	(PYANo)	(metso PYANo)	(metso FORtay)	(FORtay)	(forTISSimo)

The word **crescendo** (creSHENdo) means to gradually get louder. The symbol ——◁ means to gradually get louder.

The word **diminuendo** (diminuENDo) or **decrescendo** (decreSHENdo) means to gradually get softer. The symbol ▷—— means to gradually get softer.

Oh! Susanna (Always look at the key signature before playing a song. The one flat means that it is in the key of F; all B's are played as B♭'s.)

Oh, I come from Al - a - bam - a with a ban - jo on my knee, and I'm

goin' to Lou' - si - an - a my___ true love for to see. It___

rained all night the day I left, the weath - er it was dry, the___

sun so hot I froze to death; Su - san - na don't you cry.

Oh, Su - san - na, oh, don't you cry for me! 'Cause I

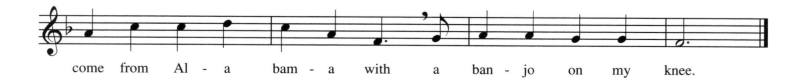

come from Al - a bam - a with a ban - jo on my knee.

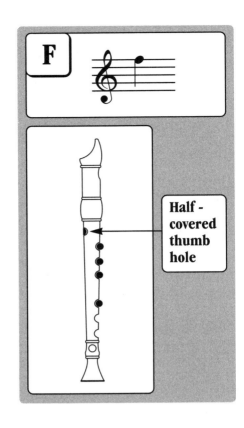

Playing High F

Like the high E you learned on page 32, high F requires that you half cover the thumb hole. The rest of the fingering is the same as the simpler fingering for middle F (page 20).

As with all higher notes on the recorder, you'll need a little more breath to make this note come out clearly.

First play the high F alone:

Then contrast it with middle F:

You'll need the high F to play this famous American folk song.

The Yellow Rose of Texas

Track 63

She's my Rose-bud, she's my Dar-lin'! My love so sweet and true! I

still can hear her laugh-ter 'neath Tex-as skies of blue. So I'm

get-tin' set to hur-ry back and I know there she'll be, my sweet

Yel-low Rose of Tex-as there a-wait-in' faith-ful-ly.

On Top of Old Smoky

Track 64

(This song is in the key of F. Remember that B's are played as B♭'s.)

Appalachian Folk Song

mp On top of Old Smok - y, all cov - ered with snow___ ___ I lost my true lov - er from court - in' too slow.___ ___ Now court - in's a plea - sure but part - ing is grief,___ ___ and a false heart - ed lov - er is worse than a thief.___

Round Her Neck She Wore a Yellow Ribbon

Track 65

This arrangement has two sets of repeat signs with 1st and 2nd endings. You may want to review page 33 for hints on how to deal with them. (Also see bottom of this page.)

Traditional

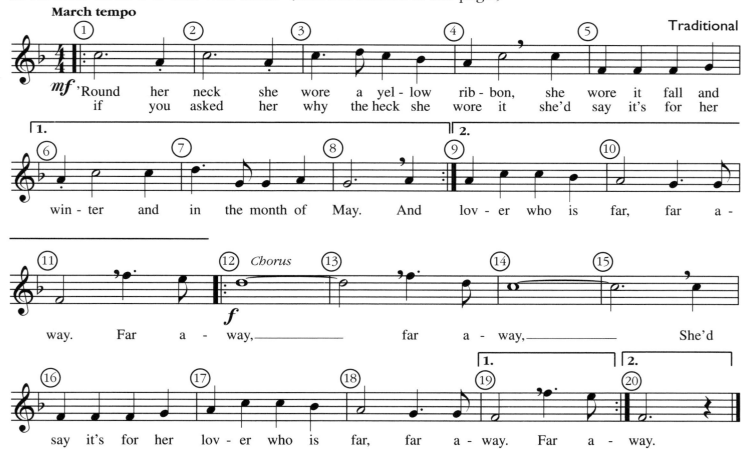

mf 'Round her neck she wore a yel - low rib - bon, she wore it fall and
if you asked her why the heck she wore it she'd say it's for her

win - ter and in the month of May. And lov - er who is far, far a-

way. Far a - way,___ far a - way,___ She'd

say it's for her lov - er who is far, far a - way. Far a - way.

Play the measures in this order: Measure 1 through 8, then 1, 2, 3, 4, 5, 9, 10, 11. Then play the chorus, measures 12 through 19, then repeat, playing 12 through 18 and finish with measure 20.

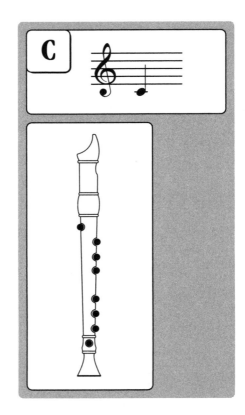

Playing Low C

This is the lowest note that can be played on the recorder. Because it requires that every hole be covered it is probably the most difficult note to produce accurately.

Be careful not to overblow; like all low notes, you should breathe gently into the mouthpiece, saying "du." Also make sure that all the holes are completely covered. Even a small opening will cause the note to play out of tune or produce an entirely different tone.

Notice that because the low C falls below the staff, a short temporary extension of the five line staff called a **leger line** is used.

The addition of the low C to our repertoire allows us to play a complete C major scale. This consists of the notes C, D, E, F, G, A, B and C as follows. (Make this scale part of your daily practice.)

The C Major Scale Track 66

Although some people think that scales are boring, it is very important to practice them for several reasons:

1. To develop speed and facility on the recorder.

2. To learn the notes in a key. The notes in the key of C are all contained in the C major scale. Therefore, if you know the scale, you'll have a much easier time playing in that key.

3. To gain facility with melodic passages that are based on scales.

Lavender's Blue Track 67

English Folk Song

THE SLUR

When two or more notes of different pitch are connected by a curved line (called a **slur**) they are played smoothly by saying the usual "du" or "tu" into the mouthpiece only once at the beginning. The tricky part is to change the fingering quickly and cleanly so that each note sounds clear.

Here's an example:

Slurred notes are very effective when playing lovely ballads such as this one. If you like, you can play the song twice, once with the slurs as written, and once with normal articulation (without the slurs).

All Through the Night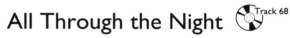

Welsh Folk Song

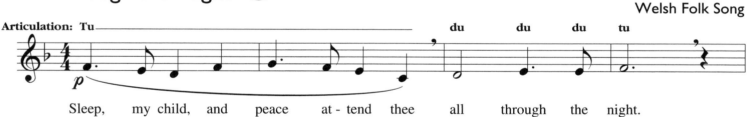

Sleep, my child, and peace at-tend thee all through the night.

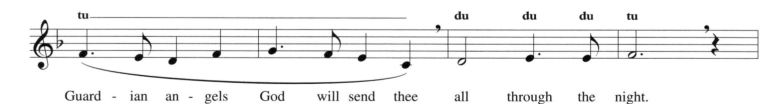

Guard-ian an-gels God will send thee all through the night.

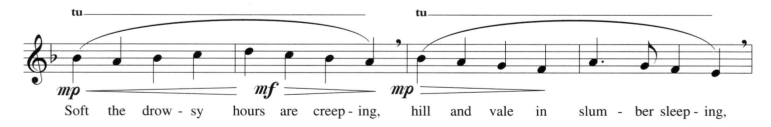

Soft the drow-sy hours are creep-ing, hill and vale in slum-ber sleep-ing,

I my lov-ing vig-il keep-ing all through the night.

ARTICULATION

You now have three different ways of articulating musical notes:

1. Normal articulation means saying "tu" or "du" into the mouthpiece, once for each note.

2. Staccato articulation means saying "tut" or "dut" into the mouthpiece, once for each note with a dot over or under it.

3. Slurred articulation, also referred to by the Italian word legato (leGAHto), which means saying "tu" or "du" into the mouthpiece only once for each group of slurred notes.

Compare and play the following:

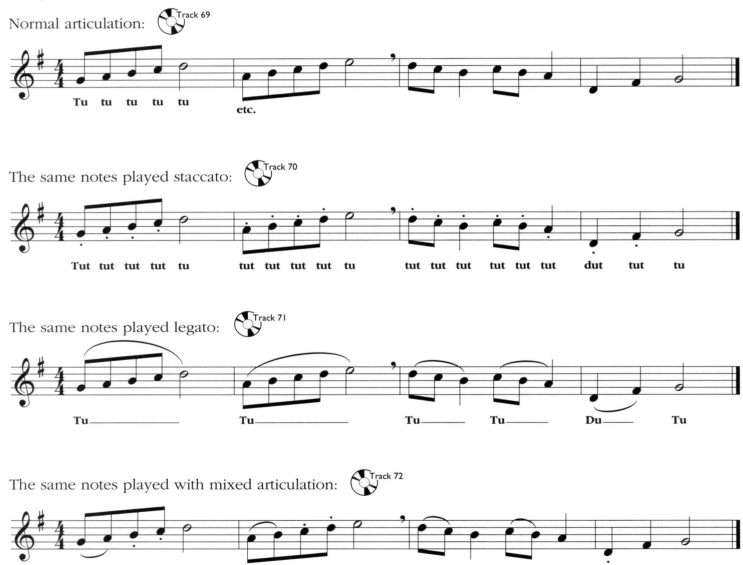

As you can hear, each articulation has a different musical effect. If you are careful in following the written articulations in music, you'll find that your playing will gain a great deal in variety, beauty and in its ability to evoke an emotional response from your listeners.

This beautiful English folk song makes use of a variety of articulations as well as giving us practice on the low C.

The Ash Grove

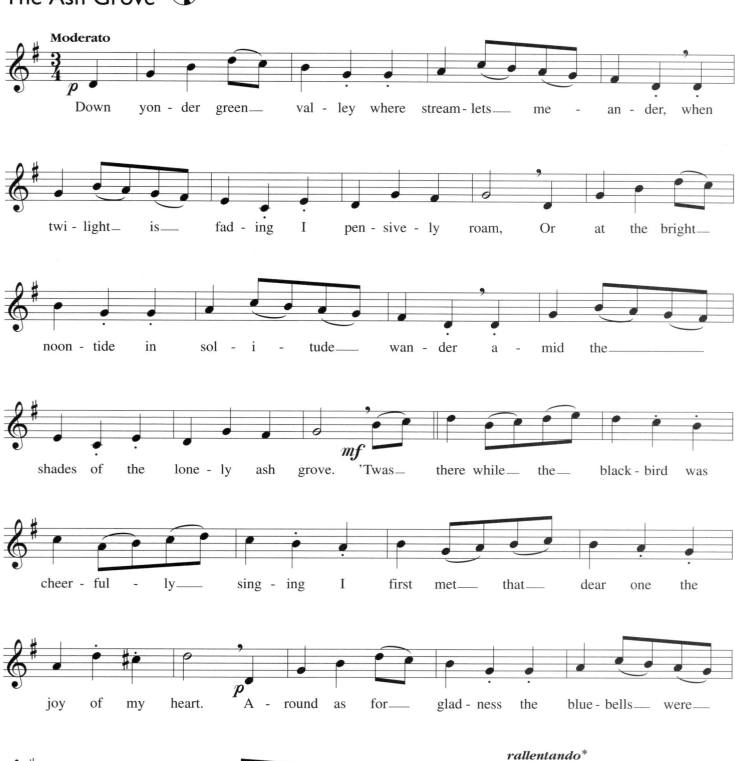

Down yon-der green— val-ley where stream-lets— me - an-der, when
twi-light— is— fad-ing I pen-sive-ly roam, Or at the bright—
noon-tide in sol-i-tude— wan-der a - mid the—
shades of the lone-ly ash grove. 'Twas— there while— the— black-bird was
cheer-ful-ly— sing-ing I first met— that— dear one the
joy of my heart. A-round as for— glad-ness the blue-bells— were—
ring-ing, Ah! then lit-tle— thought I how soon we should part.

Rallentando is an Italian word that means "slowing down." It is often used toward the end of a piece of music.

6/8 TIME Part I: Slow to Moderate

Because 6/8 time is used to notate two different styles of music, many aspiring musicians are confused about how to play it.

First of all, the "8" in the 6/8 time signature means that, unlike the 2/4, 3/4, and 4/4 you have learned, the eighth note now receives one full beat.

Songs played from a slow to moderate tempo in 6/8 time should be counted "in six," that is, six beats per measure.

Here are some fragments of familiar tunes that should be counted in six:

Drink to Me Only with Thine Eyes

Un Canadien Errant

Blow the Man Down

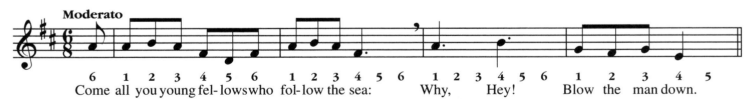

Oh Dear, What Can the Matter Be?

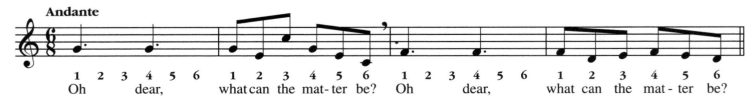

Sweet Betsy from Pike  Track 74

Oh, don't you re-mem-ber sweet Bet-sy from Pike? Who crossed the big moun-tains with

her lov-er Ike. With two yoke of ox-en, a big yal-ler dog, a tall Shang-hai roos-ter and

one spot-ted hog. Ho-dle dang fol-de di do hodle dang fol-de day.

In 6/8 time a dotted 8th note gets 1 ½ beats

1 2 & 3 4 5 6   1 2 & 3 4 5 6   1 2 & 3 4 5 & 6   1 2 3 4 5 6

Silent Night  Track 75

Words by Joseph Mohr
Music by Franz Gruber

Gently

Si - lent night, Ho - ly night, All is calm, all is bright.

Round yon Vir - gen Moth - er and child, Ho - ly in - fant so ten - der and mild,

Sleep in heav - en-ly peace; Sleep in heav - en-ly peace.

6/8 TIME Part II: Moderate Fast to Very Fast

As the tempo of 6/8 time gets faster, it becomes more difficult to count in six. Any tempo quicker than moderato should be counted "in two." This means that each beat will contain three eighth notes. Put another way, each measure of 6/8 time will contain the equivalent two groups of three eighth notes each.

Here are some fragments of familiar folk songs and marches in which the 6/8 time should be counted in two:

Pop Goes the Weasel

Traditional

When Johnny Comes Marching Home

Louis Lambert (Patrick S. Gilmore)

When John-ny comes march-ing home a-gain, hur-rah!_____ Hur-rah!_____

Lazy Mary, Will You Get Up?

Children's Song

La-zy Ma-ry, will you get up, will you get up, will you get up?

The Farmer in the Dell

Traditional

For He's A Jolly Good Fellow

Track 76

Traditional

Allegro

mf For he's a jol - ly good fel - low, for he"s a jol - ly good fel - low, for

he's a jol - ly good fel - low which no - bod - y can de - ny._____

Fine

D.C. al Fine*

Which no - bod - y can de - ny,_____ which no - bod - y can de - ny,_____

*D.C. al Fine—see footnote on page 24.

Vive l'amour
(Long Live Love)

Track 77

Traditional

Allegro

mf Let ev - 'ry good fel - low now join in a song: *f* Vi - ve la com - pag -

nie!_____ *mf* Suc - cess to each oth - er and pass it a - long: *f* Vi - ve la com - pag -

nie!_____ *f* Vi - ve la, vi - ve la, vi - ve l'a-mour, vi - ve la, vi - ve la,

vi - ve l'a-mour, vi - ve l'a-mour, vi - ve l'a-mour, vi - ve la com - pag - nie!_____

THE DOTTED 8th & 16th NOTE RHYTHM

Like eighth notes in 2/4, 3/4, or 4/4 time, dotted eighths and sixteenths are played two to each beat. But unlike eighth notes (which are played evenly) dotted eighths and sixteenths are played unevenly: long, short; long, short.

Compare the following:

8th notes:
Count: 1 & 2 & 3 & 4 &

16th notes:
Count: 1 e & a 2 e & a   etc.

Dotted 8ths and 16ths:
Count: 1 e & a 2 e & a 3 e & a 4 e & a

An easy way to remember the sound of dotted eighths and sixteenths is to say the words:

"Hump - ty Dump - ty Hump - ty Dump - ty."

Here are some fragments of familiar tunes that will help you remember the sound of dotted eighths and sixteenths:

Down by the Station

Traditional

Allegretto*

1   2 & a 1   2   1 & a 2 & a 1   2

Boogie Style

Traditional

Moderato

Taps

Army bugle call

Largo**

Allegretto is a tempo indication faster than *Andante* but slower than *Allegro*.
**Largo* means to play very slowly.

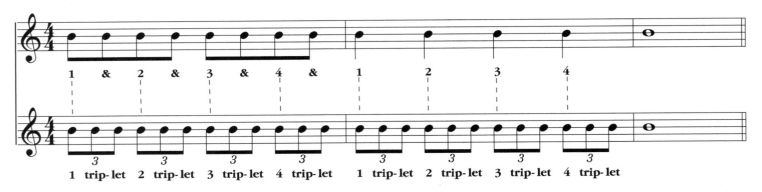

TRIPLETS

When three notes are grouped together with the figure "3" above or below the notes, the group is called a triplet. The three notes then have a rhythmic value which is the same as two of the same notes. For example, three eighth notes under a triplet sign get the same number of beats as two ordinary eighth notes, or one beat.

Compare the eighth notes and quarter notes in the first line with the triplets in the second line.

Here are some fragments of familiar tunes that will help you remember the sound of triplets:

Row, Row, Row Your Boat

Andante

Traditional

Mer - ri - ly, mer - ri - ly, mer - ri - ly, mer - ri - ly, life is but a dream.

"Triumphal March" from *Aida*

Maestoso*

Giuseppe Verdi

Someone's in the Kitchen with Dinah

Moderato

Traditional

Fee Fi, Fid-dle-de I O, Fee Fi Fid-dle-de I O

Serenade

Moderato

Franz Scubert

p

Maestoso (my-es-TO-so) means to play slowly and majestically.

56